MEET ARZEEN™

CITIZEN OF THE WORLD

By Karen Allison Shariati

Illustrations by Jay Jiyeon Kim

arZana™

Published by Arzana, Inc. (www.arzanaworld.com) in Potomac, Maryland, USA

ISBN-10: 0-9770475-0-4

ISBN-13: 978-0-9770475-0-5

Library of Congress Control Number: 2005906813

Printed in Tehran, Iran by Abyaneh Printing Org.

First Print 2006

First Edition

10 9 8 7 6 5 4 3 2 1

To My Behnam, Arzeen, and Ariana

... My World

Hello!
Please allow me to introduce myself.
My name is ARZEEN and I am a
'Citizen of the World'.

With the world at our finger tips, please join me as I travel from continent to continent. Together, we will meet people from around the globe and learn about the countries they call home.

Before we plan our journey, I would like you to meet my loyal and faithful companion. He is my lovebird, Beza, and he is always watching over me. However, he is a bit sneaky at times, flying off on his own.

Be sure to keep an eye out for Beza!

I will travel place to place crossing each continental border.
First, Australia (Oceania), Asia, Europe, and Africa,
then North America, South America, and Antarctica ...
in exactly that order.

Where will you travel first?
Will you follow my path or create your own?
Explore, discover, and have fun ...
make sure to watch for each time zone.

Expand your world and discover a new country each day!

Travel with me or skip to the destination of your choice.

commonwealth of
australia

Native Australian
(Aboriginal) Flag

capital - canberra

The Outback

Kangaroos

Crocodile

Eucalyptus Tree

Koala Bears

Frilled Neck
Lizard

G'day Mates!

Here I am south of
the equator in the
land Down Under.
In the heart of
Australia's Outback,
I am with my new
friends, the
Aborigines. With
visions of
"Dreamtime",
they are teaching
me the art of rock
painting. As many
do, the Aborigines
express their beliefs
through art and dance.

"Dreamtime" - According to the Aborigines, the time when the world, including its peoples and animals, was created.

After crossing desert, grasslands, and forests, I am splashing through an underwater world of brilliant colors. For over 1,200 miles, endless varieties of fish and coral life thrive in Australia's Great Barrier Reef.

Coral Sea

Great Barrier Reef
One of the Seven Natural Wonders

Look closely ... do you see a grand yacht ready to set sail across the Pacific Ocean? Well, it may look like a yacht, but it is actually Australia's home to music and arts, the Sydney Opera House. Take a moment to listen to the wonderful music filling the air.

Sydney Opera House

Bottlenose Dolphin

Pacific Ocean

Green Turtle

Humpback Whale

Ta Ta Australia!

new zealand
capital - wellington

Tasman Sea

"Kia ora tatou" (Hello everyone!)

Arriving in a canoe just as the Maori people migrated from the Pacific Islands, I am going to perform a Powhiri (a formal greeting) in the Poupou at Waitangi.

Poupou at Waitangi

A spear in one hand and a peace branch in the other, I approach a young Maori girl and place the peace branch on the ground. Touching our faces together, we formally greet each other according to the Maori tradition.

L&P® Soda

Tuatara

Koru
(Silver Fern)

Here I am sitting at the base of one of New Zealand's many volcanoes. Sipping my L&P® soda just like a "Kiwi" (a New Zealander), I look around and marvel at the beautiful landscape and unique animal and plant life.

Glaciers, mountain ranges, beaches, and subtropic forests ... New Zealand's terrain takes so many forms. Not to mention, there is living proof of dinosaurs right here. That's right ... the Tuatara is the only beak-headed reptile that did not become extinct 65 million years ago.

Hector's Dolphin

Pacific Ocean

As I leave New Zealand, I am lucky enough to catch a glimpse of one of the world's rarest dolphins, the Hector's Dolphin.

people's republic of
china

capital - Beijing

Happy New Year!

I arrived just in time for the Festival of Lanterns ... the final day of the Chinese New Year celebration. For the last 15 days, families and friends have gathered to celebrate good fortune, happiness, and wealth. And, of course, the decorative lanterns hanging in the streets represent the return of light and the coming of spring.

Chinese New Year Celebration

As the Festival of Lanterns comes to an end, the mighty dragon comes out of hibernation and spreads good fortune.

Each Chinese New Year is given the name of one of 12 animals. I was born in the year of the golden dragon. Which Chinese New Year were you born in?

Forbidden City

Temple of Heaven

Great Wall

Azaleas

Plum Blossoms

Panda Bear

Beza and I are traveling across China with our new friend, Panda. Together, we will climb the highest peaks of the Himalayan Mountains, cross plateaus, and hike through basins and plains. Our travels will be like a journey through history as we visit ancient landmarks. We will even follow the "silk road" as many past travelers did while trading silk and other valuable merchandise.

Red Crowned Crane

Beza and I just dropped off Panda at a bamboo forest habitat, and it is now time for us to take our next journey. As I maneuver my fishing boat down the river, I surely hope Beza catches up with me.

REPUBLIC OF
INDIA

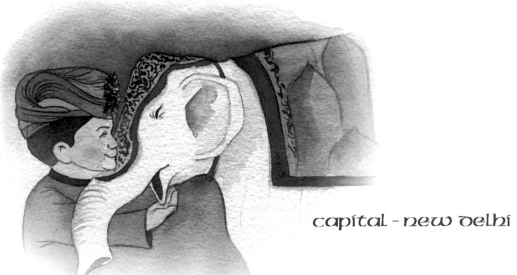

capital - new delhi

Mehndi
(Henna Designs)

Bhavai Dancer

Rangoli

With great honor, I accept the invitation to my friend's wedding. Around the world, the marriage ceremony is a sacred custom, and India is no exception. In India, the wedding traditions vary by region, but one thing remains constant, the wedding ceremony is the most important event in the lives of the bride and groom, as well as their families.

Mandap

Roses and Marigolds

Wedding Ceremony

Taj Mahal

Peacock Feathers, Flowers, and Curry

Tiger

Snake Charmer

To say India is filled with beauty is an understatement. From the grand peaks of the Himalayan Ranges to the amazing coastline surrounded by three bodies of water, India's nature is a gift to your eyes. Not to mention, India's land is graced with beautiful buildings ... none more spectacular than the Taj Mahal. While the architectural style of this wonder can be traced back to Central Asia, Persia, and Islam, the true inspiration for its construction was an emperor's memory of his loving wife.

Red Panda

Dromedary Camel

12

islamic republic of íran

Norouz (New Year) Decorations

capital - tehran

"Norouz-tan Mobarak" (Happy New Year).

Ibex

Khaju Bridge

Imam Mosque

Tea House

Pistachio Tree

Persian Cat

Silver Work

Haji Firouz

Isfahan

It is the first day of spring, the first day of the new year, and together we are celebrating new beginnings, health, fertility, and wealth for the coming year. I have never felt as at home as I do here in Isfahan, but when one considers the Persian way of life, it is not so difficult to believe. Persians open their hearts as well as their homes to all, and not just during Norouz, but each and every day of their lives. The people of Iran live to share life with one another, whether it is dancing to music, sitting down for a wonderful meal, or drinking chai-ee (tea) with saffron. The Persian spirit and culture are very old, but remain ever so strong.

13

From the Caspian Sea to the Persian Gulf, Iran is over flowing with architectural wonders, none more impressive than Persepolis. Once thought of as the "richest city under the sun", Persepolis was a capital city of the powerful Persian Empire. Founded by Cyrus the Great and further developed by Darius the Great, Persepolis was a city ahead of its time, until its devastating destruction by the Greek king, Alexander the Great.

Azadi Tower, Tehran

Ahura Mazda

Gate of all Nations, Takt-e-Jamshid (Persepolis)

While the grand Persepolis is now in ruins, the legacy of great rulers lives on in the people of Iran as well as the world. A perfect example, from nearly 2,500 years ago, is the legacy of Cyrus the Great. He ruled with compassion and understanding for different cultures and religious beliefs ... it is hard to believe, but all those years ago, he created the first human rights.

RUSSIAN
federation

Crocus Biflorus

capital - moscow

Welcome to the biggest country in the world! From village life in Siberia to city life in imperial St. Petersburg, this country is culturally diverse. Russia spans two continents, Europe and Asia, and elever (count them, eleven) time zones. And, did you know that eastern Russia is only 50 miles away from North America. No wonder people and animals migrated back and forth throughout history.

Siberia

Yak

The Mariinsky Theatre

Peter and Paul Fortress

Peter the Great Monument

St. Petersburg

15

While in St. Petersburg, my schedule will be quite busy. First, I will be heading to one of the largest art galleries in the world, and then I will see the ballet, Swan Lake.

St. Basil's Cathedral

Red Square, Moscow

Victory Day Parade in Red Square

While I came to Moscow to see the colors and shapes of the infamous St. Basil's Cathedral, I also came to take part in a very important ceremony. In the presence of some of the world's greatest leaders, I marched with the Russian military to proudly honor all those who were dedicated to a World War II victory. As we move to the future ... a future based on cultural awareness, it is important to understand our history and how it shaped our world and its peoples.

Trans-Siberian Railway

Siberian Husky

Here we go, Beza, crossing Russia on the Trans-Siberian Railway. Being the longest railroad in the world, it is going to take us days to make this trip.

republic of

turkey

Ottoman Military Drummer

capital - ankara

I am here at the Grand Bazaar and ready to shop. This is one of the largest covered markets in the world and it is filled with jewelry, spices, and much, much more. The charm of the bazaar is granc, although it is no match for the charm of the people within the Grand Bazaar.

Grand Bazaar, Istanbul

Rugs, Fabrics, and Jewelry

These dancers traveled from southeastern Turkey and are performing a traditional folk dance. As in many cultures, folk dances tell a story. This story is about cultivating the land.

The city of Istanbul is truly where East meets West. The city is divided by two continents, Asia on the east side and Europe on the west side. And, I can tell you first hand, that the city is a wonderful mix of both. From the city's architecture to culture, you can definitely see the influences of both continents.

Bald Ibis

WEST · EAST
EUROPE · ASIA

Van Cat

Bosphorus Straits

Kangal Dog

Mediterranean Monk Seal

Blue Mosque

Loggerhead Turtle

Sea of Marmara

It won't be long now, Beza. The Sea of Marmara will lead us to the Aegean Sea.

Excuse me, what was that you said, Beza? Oh! I thought I told you we are heading to Greece.

Loggerhead Turtle

Sea of Marmara

Tulips

18

Statue of Zeus at Olympia
One of the Seven Wonders of the Ancient World

hellenic republic
greece

capital - athens

The first Olympics, the Ancient Olympic Games, were held in honor of the god Zeus, the supreme Goc of Greek mythology. The ancient games were held every four years starting in 776 BC and continuing for nearly 1,200 years. People came from all over the Greek world and some from beyond the Greek borders to join the Olympic festivals.

Mount Olympus

Ancient and Modern Olympics

For the last 100 years or so, our world once again is fortunate to have the Olympic Games. The modern games now stretch far beyond the borders of the ancient Greek world. Men and women from around the world compete together. Just another example of how the people of our world are connected.

19

Peacock Anemone

Iris Pumila

Tree Frog

Green Toad

Greater Periwinkle

Elenoras Falcon

Parthenon, Athens

Socrates

Hippocrates

I wish I could travel back in time to relive the stories of Greek mythology and to talk with the great philosophers of ancient times. These stories and philosophies, in many ways, shaped modern life in Greece and around the world. For instance, Hippocrates, a Greek physician, educated many with his medical findings and is credited with the Hippocratic Oath, which is still followed by doctors today. And, Socrates, a Greek philosopher, taught many of us about ethics, virtue, and knowledge.

Greek Pottery

Horse and Chariot

Excuse me ... did you happen to see where Beza flew off to?

20

united kingdom of
great britain

Grenadier Guards

Good day old chap!

Riding upstairs in a double-decker bus, I am touring London's hot spots ... and, there are many. I just went to St. James's Palace, and then Buckingham Palace to watch the Changing of the Guard ceremony. I had my eye out for Her Majesty the Queen, but no luck, I was only able to spot her at Madame Tussauds Wax Museum. So, now here I am in Piccadilly Circus, the junction of five busy streets. This major London landmark is filled with business people, shoppers, tourists, and most of all, it is filled with life and excitement.

St. Mary-le-Bow Church
(Home of the Bow Bells)

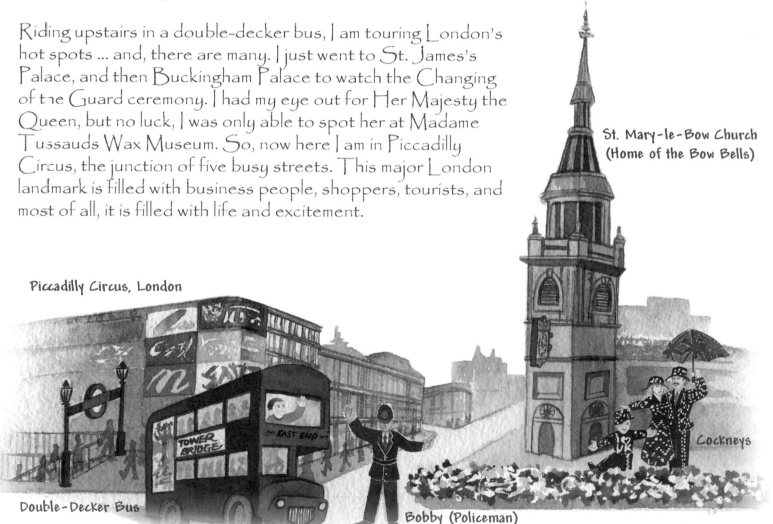

Piccadilly Circus, London

Double-Decker Bus

Bobby (Policeman)

Cockneys

While I certainly was not born within the sound of the Bow Bells, today, I am a regular Cockney. As such, I am dressed in pearl-trimmed clothes with even my 'tit for tat' covered in pearls. By the way, for those of you who do not speak Cockney, when I say 'tit for tat', I mean 'hat'.

After protecting the crown jewels at the Tower of London, I am cruising up the Old Coast Road into the heart of Northumberland. There are so many stops to make ... one of my favorites being the Roman-built Hadrian's Wall. Northumberland is graced with so very many beautiful castles, Warkworth, Alnwick, and Berwick to name a few, but my all time personal favorite is Bamburgh Castle.

Farne Island Puffins

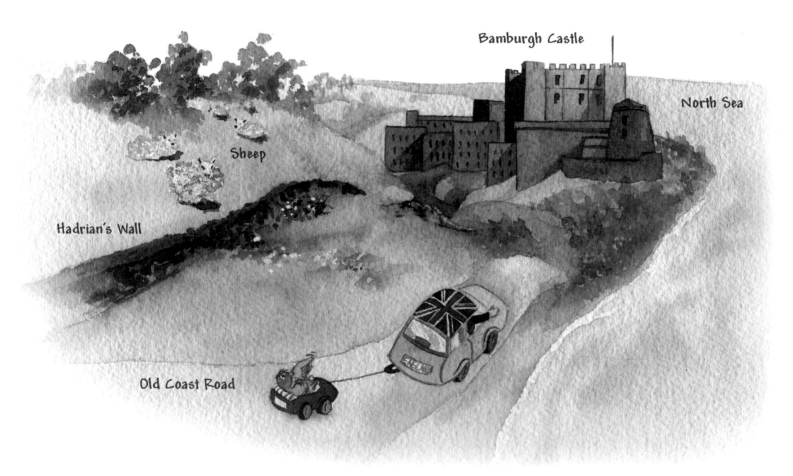

Bamburgh Castle

North Sea

Sheep

Hadrian's Wall

Old Coast Road

Beza, where did you find that little car? You are always up to something ... eeeh you cheeky monkey.

Tara (Good Bye) U.K.

Raven

Tower of London, River Thames, London

Yeomen Warders ("Beefeaters")

22

italian
republic

capital - rome

Ciao! Greetings from the capital of Italy. Amph theatres were not unique to the Roman Empire, but none were as magnif cent and grand as the Colosseum in Rome. Can you imagine what it would have been like to be a spectator watching animal fighting and gladiator combat?

Flavian Amphitheatre (Colosseum), Rome

St. Peter's Basilica, Vatican City

Swiss Guards Corps

Do you know where the smallest nation in the world is located?

Well, I am sure you guessed Rome, but do you know the name of this independent state? That's right ... the Vatican City, home to about 1,000 people and some of Michelangelo's greatest works of art. Protected by the Swiss Guards, the Vatican City welcomes many, many visitors each year.

23

Maneuvering my gondola down the Grand Canal, it is easy to understand why so many visitors travel great lengths to reach Venice ... the busy marketplace in the Rialto Bridge, outdoor cafes, a gondolier serenading a couple in love. The list goes on and on, but one thing is for sure, Venice is an amazing city. Venice is made up of over 100 islands separated by narrow canals and connected by bridge after bridge.

Italian Spinone

Pheasant

Rialto Bridge

Gondola

Grand Canal, Venice

Ahhhh! When I think of Venice, my thoughts are of amore (love). Speaking of love, where did Beza fly off to this time?

For now, Arrivederci (Bye bye)!

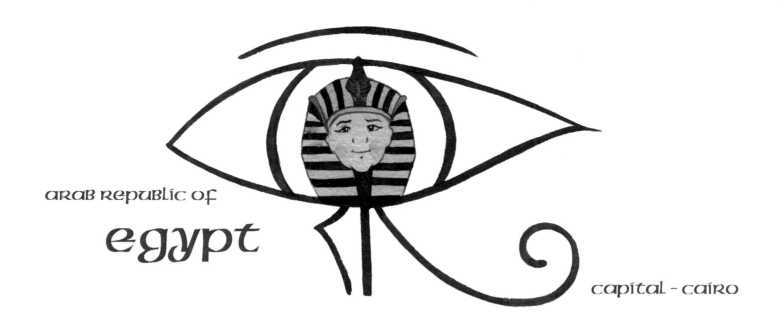

ARAB REPUBLIC OF
egypt

CAPITAL - CAIRO

Okay, maybe you can help me out a little bit. What do you know about Egyptian hieroglyphics? Well, as I read, or try to read, this ancient map of the port of Alexandria, visions of days long ago come to mind. Ancient days when the port was lit by the legendary lighthouse. A time when Alexandria was the center of learning, not to mention the very spot where Cleopatra and Mark Antony made history. One thing is for sure, I should have brushed up on my hieroglyphics.

The Lighthouse of Alexandria
One of the Seven Wonders of the Ancient World

Port of Alexandria
Eastern Harbour, Mediterranean Sea

Pillar of Pompeii

Map Written on Papyrus
(Ancient Paper)

25

The builders of the Giza Pyramids were much more than architects, they were visionaries. Built thousands of years ago, these pyramids were monumental tombs for the pharaohs, or kings, of Egypt. Without modern machinery, thousands of men erected the pyramids. To say that this was an incredible accomplishment is a bit of an understatement, huh?

You will never believe how much thought went into the design and location of these pyramids. Aligned with the stars and planets, the pyramids represent the rays of the sun. They were built on the west bank of the River Nile since the sun sets on the west bank ... in the land of the dead.

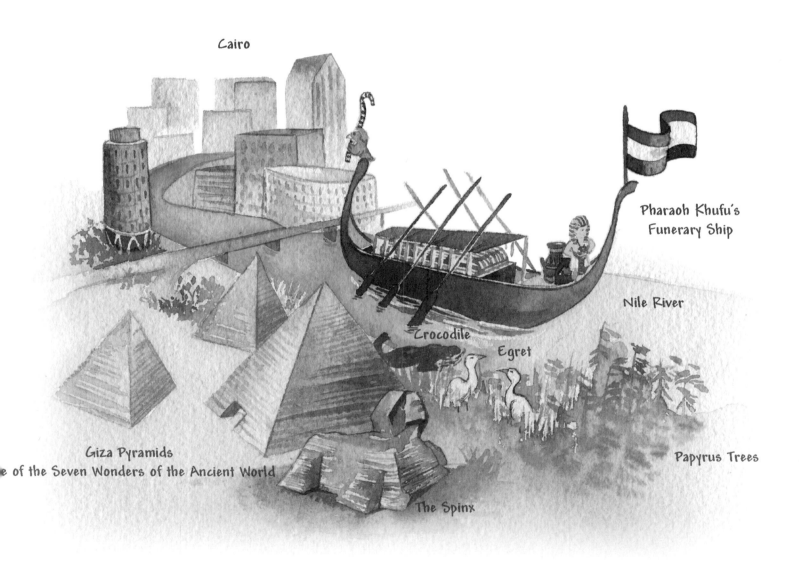

Cairo

Pharaoh Khufu's Funerary Ship

Nile River

Crocodile

Egret

Giza Pyramids
e of the Seven Wonders of the Ancient World

Papyrus Trees

The Spinx

Beza, do you realize how significant it is to be able to see the Giza pyramids? Well, out of the seven wonders of the ancient world, none of them are still standing except for the pyramids.

Uh oh! Beza, did you hear something? Was it my imagination or is that mummy coming back to life?

26

REPUBLIC OF
south africa

capitals - pretoria,
Bloemfontein
and cape town

From the southern part of the African continent, atop of Table Mountain, I look off into the distance. My interest quickly turns into fascination, so I make my way to the Zulu Nation.

Cape Floral Kingdom

KwaZulu Natal (Zulu Nation)

Table Mountain, Cape Town

Atlantic Ocean

The Zulu people are a proud and impressive group. Originally a warrior people, able to hunt and live off of the land, they believe strongly in the knowledge of their elders and ancestors. My visit to KwaZulu Natal showed me just how many reasons there are to be amazed with the Zulu. However, two things fascinated me the most.

First, their love of their culture and traditions. Did you know that the Zulu regularly hold celebrations to revive their culture and traditions? Second, the infamous brightly colored bead work. While the bead work presents beautiful geometric patterns that were made by hand, I am more impressed by the fact that the bead work is a code system. Did you hear me? The bead design is actually a code. By combining specific colors in a certain way, a message is created within the geometric pattern. This is their own unique communication system.

27

Lion

Leopard

Hippopotamus

Zebra

Elephant

Buffalo

Shhhh! I am taking a safari ride through Kruger National Park. This is nature at its best. Not only am I in South Africa's infamous flora region, I am witnessing the "Big Five" in action. That's right ... South Africa's big five, the lion, leopard, elephant, rhinoceros, and buffalo, are right here. They were once endangered by hunters, but within this nature reserve, the big five ... well, they thrive.

Giraffe

28

kingdom of **MOROCCO**

capital - RABAT

Al sa aam a'alaykum (Good day)! Upon my arrival, I was surprised to find out that Casablanca is quite a modern city. In fact, it is the largest city in Morocco and it is a center of industry. My vision of the city was quite different. So, I went on a mission to discover the Casablanca that I had seen in movies and read about in books.

Hassan II Mosque

Ancient Medina (Old Quarters) in City of Casablanca

My mission led me to the Old Quarters where the streets are filled with life and a plethora of colors, and the alleyways are the narrowest I ever saw. I am fascinated with the rugs, pottery, and other hand-made crafts. Would you like a souvenir?

29

A trip to Casablanca would not be complete without a visit to Hassan II Mosque. To be honest, you cannot go to Casablanca without seeing it ... its tower, or minaret, is 210 meters high and can be seen for miles.

Now that I made my way up the coast from Casablanca to Tangier, I realize just how close the continent of Africa is to the continent of Europe. I feel like I could almost touch the rock of Gibraltar, the big rocky peninsula on the southern coast of Spain. Keep one thing in mind, Gibraltar is actually a colony of the United Kingdom.

Kasbah, Tangier

Lemon Tree

Cous-Cous Meal in Courtyard

While sightseeing, some new friends invited me for an early afternoon meal, the main meal of the day. We are eating cous-cous with our hands while seated on the floor in their courtyard, the center of their home. Well, I should correct myself ... to say the courtyard is the center of their home does not quite accurately define 'courtyard' according to the Moroccan people. The courtyard is much more than that, it is the center of life.

Gazelle

Fennec Fox

Hold on a minute ... if we are going to make it to North America, then we are going the wrong way. The airport is this way!

Horned Viper

30

canada

capital - ottawa

Rocky Mountains

Inuit People

Snow Houses (Igloos)

Polar Bear

Caribou

Dog Sled

Grizzly Bear

Salmon

Moose

Ta Da Da Dum ...
Ta Da Da Dum ...
the Inuit people, once known as
Eskimos, are performing a drum dance
to welcome me to their land.
The Inuit live in the Arctic
regions of Canada and came
from as far off as Alaska and northeastern Russia. They hunt for their food
and make traditional clothes from fur, seal skin, or caribou hide.

31

You will never believe it, but Canada made me an honorary Mountie. Now Beza and I can help the second largest country in the world. Since Canada is so spread out, it will take many of us Mounties to do the job. Fortunately, most of Canada's people live in the more southern regions ... where it is not so icy and frigid.

Canada is an incredibly beautiful country with strong French and British influences. And, in recent years, Canada has close connections to the United States of America and Mexico. Together, these three North American countries created the world's largest trading area. It is amazing what we can accomplish when we work together.

Canada's Houses of Parliament
and Rideau Canal, Ottawa

Canada Geese

Arctic Fox

Royal Canadian Mounted Police

Maple Tree

While riding on horseback with my fellow Mounties, I could not resist picking a maple leaf from one of the trees. After all, the maple leaf is a national emblem.

united states of america

Kokopelli

Bald Eagle

capital - washington, d.c.

Bald Eagle

Seattle Space Needle

Delicate Arch in Arches
National Park, Utah

Wolf

Long before Europeans explored and
colonized the United States of America,
Native Americans made their homes in canyons,
grasslands, and even cliffs. Join me and climb
down the ladder ... we are invited to a pow wow.

Kokopelli

Cliff Dwelling in Mesa Verde
National Park, Colorado

33

Dressed in colorful, hand-made clothing, the Native Americans perform a
spiritual dance to music. Honoring their ancestors, the ceremony shares
stories of their past.

From coast to coast, from natural wonders to sky
scrapers, the United States of America is a diverse
and beautiful land. As I travel from west to east, one
thing becomes quite clear. This country is made up of a
collection of the peoples of the world. There is not one
culture here, rather there are many, many unique cultures
sharing this country.

Empire State Building

New York, NY

Statue of Liberty

The Washington Monument

Washington, D.C.

The Lincoln Memorial

The Jefferson
Memorial

The Capitol Building

Potomac River

Cherry Blossom Tree

Come along with me ... I am riding my bike along the Potomac River. It will
not be long before we reach Mount Vernon, the home of this country's
first president, George Washington.

REPUBLIC OF

panama

capital - panama city

Ahoy Matey!

Panama, once considered a far off land in the Americas, was a vision of treasures to pirates sailing these tropical waters. As Spaniards loaded gold and silver on ships heading for Spain, sea raiders were waiting at sea. This beautiful land of natural resources endured further hardship as Sir Henry Morgan of England destroyed Panama La Vieja in the hopes of acquiring Spanish findings. With a strong spirit, the people of Panama rebuilt the city nearby naming it "Old City".

Panama La Vieja
(Old Panama)

Caribbean Sea

Papaya Tree

Kuna Indians

Old City

Among the natives, the Kuna Indians thrive growing their own crops, hunting, creating pottery and other works of art, and living in thatch roof huts.

During my visit, many locals talked about the Isthmus of Panama. Do you know what "isthmus" means? Well, an isthmus is a narrow strip of land that is bordered on two sides by water and connects two larger land masses. Okay, based on this definition, is Panama an isthmus? That's right ... Panama is a narrow strip of land that is bordered by the Caribbean Sea and the Pacific Ocean and connects two larger land masses, North America and South America.

The Isthmus of Panama became the perfect location for a canal, so the Panama Canal was developed. Now, ships can travel through Panama rather than going all the way around Cape Horn, the southernmost tip of South America. Just imagine how this changed the lives of all Panamanians as well as the people of the world.

Panama City

Toucan

Panama Canal

Beza ... Beza, please take a break from sun bathing and help me out. Do you know who helped Panama construct the canal? Oh, thanks Beza. I did not realize the United States of America helped Panama.

36

FEDERATIVE REPUBLIC OF BRAZIL

The Emergent Layer

Amazon Rainforest

Azara Azul

Before arriving in Brazil, I thought and thought about where I should visit first. And, then it was clear ... so, here I am in the Amazon Rainforest, home to some of the most unique species in the world. From atop an emergent tree, I am examining the countless types of animals and plants. The rainforest has already provided our world with medical miracles, and I am certain there are many more miracles to be found.

The Canopy Layer

The Understory Layer

The Forest Floor Layer

Jaguar

Tapir

Yanomamo Tribe

Boa Constrictor

While mankind continues to destroy the rainforest, the Yanomamo Tribe lives in harmony with the rainforest. The Yanomamo people are very primitive, yet they respect nature and all its powers. Even though many have said this before me, please "Save the Rainforest".

Municipal Theatre

Samba Parade

Carnival, Rio de Janeiro

Flashes of colors, exotic costumes, lively spirits ... all dancing to the samba beat. Yes, you guessed it, I am here in Rio de Janeiro celebrating Brazil's Carnival. People have traveled from near and far to join in the festive street parties.

It is the heart of summertime here in Rio. For those of you who are thinking it is wintertime right now ... well, you are obviously on the other side of the equator. One thing is for sure, I will be staying right here in Rio de Janeiro for this several day celebration.

38

REPUBLIC OF
chile

capital - santiago

Jump into my plane and fly with me high above the Pacific Ocean. Here we go ... flying west away from Chile's coast, we first spot the site of Robinson Crusoe's tales. Just imagine being stranded on a deserted island for several years. One thing is for sure, the landscape and flora are absolutely magical. Not to mention, the amazing hummingbirds.

Moai Statues

Easter Island

Juan Fernández Firecrown (Hummingbird)

Ochagavia elegans (Flowers)

Archipelago Juan Fernández (Robinson Crusoe Island)

South Pacific Ocean

39

As we head farther west, magic turns into mystery when we see the majestic stone statues, the Moai statues. No one quite knows who built these massive statues or how they were moved into their positions. Some of them are over 60 feet high. When I talked to the natives, they were not able to explain the origins of these statues ... the mystery continues.

From top to bottom, which is quite a stretch, Chile's land is so very diverse. Each area I visit is more impressive than the one before ... from the driest desert to the lake district, which captures reflections of the grand Andes Mountains, to Patagonia, the frozen end of South America. This spectacular land is only surpassed by the beautiful people, who live life to the fullest with style, elegance, and a bit of European flare.

Hang on, Beza! We are heading to our last stop in South America ... to Tierra Del Fuego, where we will find the southernmost settlements in the world.

antarctica

Greetings from the coldest place on earth ... the south pole. With such icy, frozen terrain, it should come as no surprise that no one makes their home in Antarctica. People do visit, but mainly to conduct research on rocks, icebergs, and animals.

Scientists
Conducting Study

46

Leopard Seals

Blue-eyed Birds

Emperor Penguins

Killer Whale

Wooohooooo! Watch me go ... I am sliding down icebergs just like the Emperor Penguins. Of course, the penguins are keeping a watchful eye out for Killer Whales and Leopard Seals. The penguins, as well as all animal life, have always had natural enemies, but now with human visitors, the future of Antarctic wildlife is uncertain. Preserving nature's balance will be of utmost importance as scientists continue to perform studies.

Weddell Seal

As I make my exit from Antarctica, take one last look. Did you notice that my snow mobile does not have a country flag attached, but rather a plain, white flag? That's right ... no one country claims Antarctica, so there is no official flag.

Check out my passport now! It is filled with stamps from the many places I visited. My adventures amazed me, and taught me a very valuable lesson:

The world is filled with so many people ... all with unique cultures and traditions. While we may speak different languages, wear different clothes, eat different foods, and even live in different types of homes, we are all from one world and we are all basically the same. It is important to cherish our unique backgrounds, but more important, to be understanding of our differences.

After all, our world is ever changing. For years, each country has been influenced by the ideas shared by past travelers. And, as we move into the future, our lives will undoubtedly become even more connected.

Please allow me to introduce my new friends ...
or, should I say, "Our new friends".

We are all 'Citizens of the World'.

Excuse me, I would like to tell you one last thing ...

Thank you! Thank you for traveling and
exploring the world with me.

Your fellow 'Citizen of the World',

ARZEEN

Name _____

Date of Birth _____

Place of Birth _____

Paste YOUR picture here!

CITIZEN OF THE WORLD

Get your passport ready
for our next journey together!